7 Laws of Color

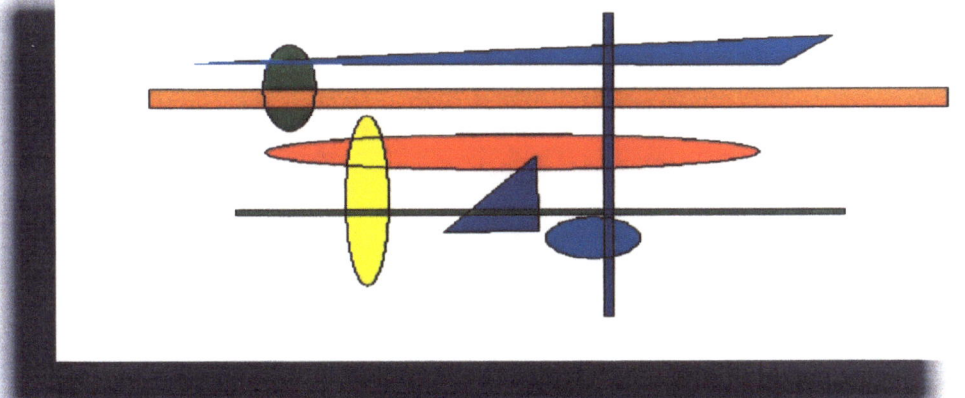

Color Simple

A new concept

Simple approach

Great results

Color is one of the most fascinating and profit generating services we can offer our clients today!

I have been an educator for several salons, color companies and cosmetology schools. What you should know about this along with other classes and books provided by this Company, is the concepts can be applied to most meager product lines on the market today.

With this proven system you can formulate most color lines. From covering gray, to fixing any color correction that sits in your chair.

We teach a simple level and tone systems Level 1-10. Level 1 is the darkest, Level 10 is the lites. Your tones are warm and cool. Red the warmest-Blue being the coolest.

We teach the 7 Laws of Color. And can tell you this. These laws don't change!

Once you have mastered these laws, the world of color will open up, and let you in!

We teach

Color Placement
Color Formulation
Color Correction
Color Trends
Color Simple Techniques
Speed technics to help with speed.
The faster you work . The more money you will make!!! So lets get started!

Chapter 1

7 Laws of Color

Law # 1 : Color won't lift color

Law # 2 : Color on top of color makes more color.

Law # 3 : porous hair will always grab cool tones.

Law # 4 : Healthy hair will show warm tones when lifting hair.

Law # 5 : To color hair back darker you must fill the hair with warmth.

Law # 6 : There are only 4 ways to color hair.

1: Darken hair

2: Lighten hair

3: Cover gray

4: Change the tone

Law #7 : There is no natural RED hair.
The hair is Orange, Yellow or variations of the two.

The laws of color does not change, and are the basics of all hair coloring.

MEMORIZE THEM

On the following pages there will be a breakdown of the 7 Laws of Color, and how they work in hair coloring!

Law # 1 : Color won't lift color
Putting a lighter hair color on a darker hair color won't lift the darker hair colors.

Law # 2 : Color + color = color
If you put hair color on color treated hair it will only change the tone, or make the hair color darker.

Law # 3 : Porous hair will always grab cool tones

If you put a neutral color on porous hair it will always grab the cool tones in the neutral hair color. Giving the hair a gray cast. You will have to fill the hair with warm tones or add warm tones to your color formula.

Law # 4 : Healthy hair will show warm tones

When lifting healthy hair you will always have warm tones to work with. These warm tones are called (residual pigment contribution) or R.P.C. for short. Each level has its own warm tone.

Law # 5 : To color hair back to a darker color you must put back what was taken out. This is called a filler. To avoid cool tones you have to fill the hair with warm tones.

Law # 6 : There are only four ways to color hair

#1 darken hair : Darkening hair in the right area will do the same thing as makeup. Giving the face a slimming affect and bring out tones in the skin.

#2 : Lighten hair : Lightening hair in certain areas will highlite tones and features in the face.

#3 : Cover gray hair : Covering gray hair is one of the most popular color services preformed in the salon today (dont forget the men).

#4 : Change the tones : Changing the tones in the hair can also change the tones in the skin and bring out tones in the eyes.

Law # 7 : There are no natural red heads.

A natural red head has orange, yellow, or a varitation of the two. So you never use green to change the tones in natural hair.
(use blue , violet or a varitation of the two)

Hopefully this chapter has helped you better understand the 7 Laws of Color. Once again, these are laws you can apply to most major color lines on the market today.

One last thing
THER ARE NO SHORTCUTS TO HAIR COLOR!

Chapter 2
The System

The system we have created uses 4 charts which you can hang in your color cabinet

#1 The level chart (swatch chart)
#2 Color wheel
#3 Under line pigment (UPC)
#4 base chart for each tonal series

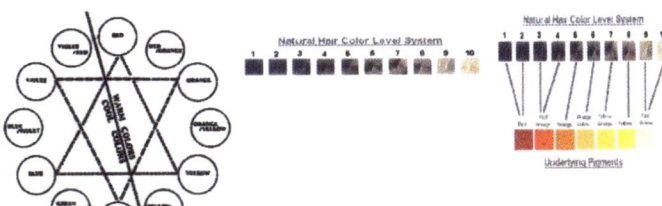

Base Chart natural /

With these 4 charts you can conquer the world of color with confidence

Now a breakdown of the 4 charts

#1 The neutral level chart or the neutral swatch chart is used to find your clients level. This is the ten level system. Level 1 being the darkest and 10 being the lighest. If you get this range your color won't come out right.

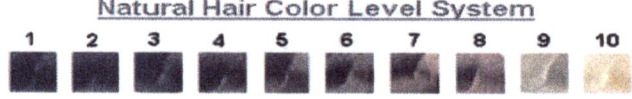

You find the neutral level by pushing the swatch into the hair or placing the chart next to the hair. If it matches, that is your level.

#2 The color wheel will tell you the neutralizing tone. The tones opposite each other will give you brown or beige.

IE orange + blue = brown

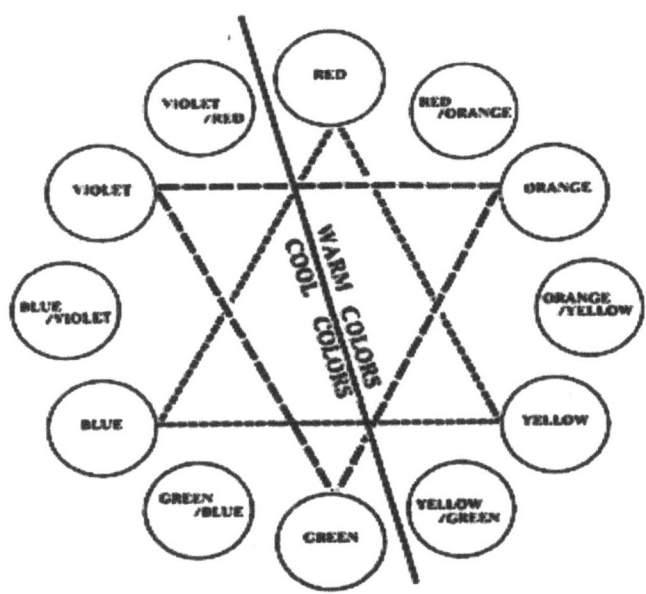

This chart is also divided into 2 sides. One side is warm tones, the other side is cool tones. This will also help with corrective color

.

#3 The underlying pigment chart will tell you what warm tones you will encounter when lifting hair. You can use this tone or neutralize them with the opposite tones on the color wheel.

If the underlying pigment is yellow, use a color with a violet base to neutralize the yellow in the hair.

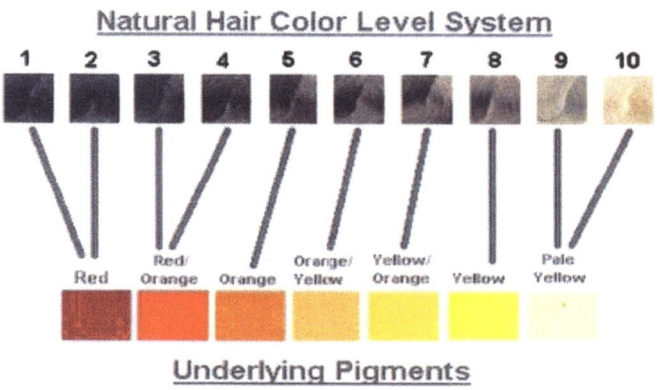

This chart will also give you the fillers to use for corrective color.

#4 Your base chart will tell you the base of each tonal series the color line offers. This helps you choose the correct tone to use to achieve your hair color goals.

Base Chart
natural / neutral
natural ash / neutral
ash / violet-blue
golden beige / gold-violet
gold / gold-yellow
warm brown / neutral-red
chocolate / gold-red
golden copper / orange
copper / orange-gold
intense copper / orange-red
red copper / orange
mahogany / red-violet
auburn / red-gold
red / red
intense red / red-red
red violet / red-violet
violet / violet

This is a must know!

Chapter 3

The Formula

The formula goes as followed:

#1 : Using your neutral swatch chart to find your customers natural level (1-10)

#2 : Find the customer desired color

#3 : Decide how many levels of lift or deposit your desired color requires. For more than 4 levels of lift you have to use bleach. this will also determine which developer to use.

Developers

10 vol. will give you deposit or 1 level of lift.
20 vol. will give you 2 levels of lift.
30 vol. will give you 3 levels of lift
40 vol. will give you 4 levels of lift

Process time

10 vol.- 20 min.
20 vol.- 30 min.
30 vol.- 40 min.
40 vol.- 50 min.

#4 Find your underlying pigment. The desired level will tell you what the UPC will be. When lifting, the UPC will tell you what warm tones you will have to neutralize or intensify.

If you are depositing color or changing the tone, the UPC will tell you what tones to use to fill porous hair before applying your desired tone.

#5 Pick a tone. The base chart will tell you the dominating tones in each tonal series. The tone is represented by the letter on the color box. The neutral series has a balance of the three primary tones.(red - blue - yellow)

#6 add your tone to your level and that's your color. The color wheel will give you your neutralizing tones

ITS THAT SIMPLE!!!
Lets color some hair!!!

Chapter 4

Color Correction

It's been said that a person doesn't learn hair color by doing hair color. They learn by fixing it.

To correct hair color you must first determine the problem. Then determine the degree to which you can fix it. (be realistic)

Color Problems

color too dark
color too light
line of demarcation
color too intense
color too drab
color has the range tones

Color too Dark

If your hair color is too dark, you must use bleach to lighten it.

If you need to lighten just the ends of the hair you can do this at the shampoo bowl. Apply a small amount of dry bleach to the darker part of the hair. Then add hot water or a clarifying shampoo to the dry bleach. You can safely get 1 level of lift with this formula.

For more lift you must use bleach with developer.(10 vol, 20 vol......)

Color too Light

If hair color is too light you must deposit hair color on the lighter hair.

If you have to deposit hair color on porous hair you must use a filler with warm tones, or add warm tones to your hair color formula.

If you are going more then 2 levels darker use filler. Less than 2 levels, add to formula.

Line of Demarcation

Each line of demarcation must be treated as its own problem. Each problem will have its own formula. The most important part of formulating is your starting point. Each line has its own starting point.

To find the starting point, use your UPC chart. If the hair is gold, it's a level 7. If it's orange, it's a level 5-6.

Determine your desired color and formulate from your starting point of each line of demarcation.

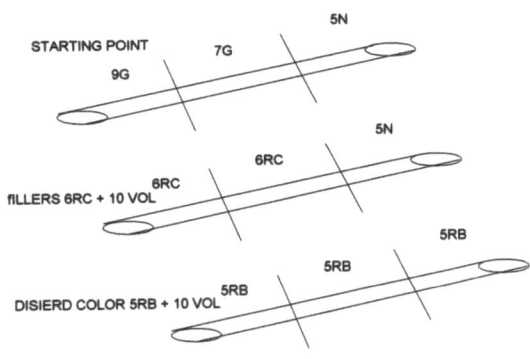

Color too Intense

If the hair color is too intense you can do a color wash with a color that is 1 level lighter with a neutral tone . This will change the tone, not the level. You should use a cool tone to make the color wash. The hair color will be less intense.

You make a color wash with 1/3 color + 1/3 10 vol + 1/3 shampoo .

Apply to wet hair at the shampoo bowl. This can take up to 20 min to finish processing.

Color too Drab

If hair color is too drab you can warm the hair color up by doing a color wash with a warm tone color .

Color has the Wrong Tone

To change the tone of a hair color you mix the desired tone 1 level lighter. This will change the tone, not the level. Mix with 10 vol. developer.

The four charts that come with this system should be at your disposal whenever you do your next hair color. They have been invaluable to me.

Thanks for your interest and your support.

Respectfully,
Fredrick Silas Bell
Fık S Bell
Color Simple

Base Chart

natural / neatral

natural ash / neatral

ash / violet-blue

golden beige / gold-violet

gold / gold-yellow

warm brown / neutral-red

chocolate / gold-red

golden copper / gold-orenge

copper / orenge-gold

intense copper / orenge-red

red copper / red-orenge

mahogany / red-violet

auburn / red-golde

red / red

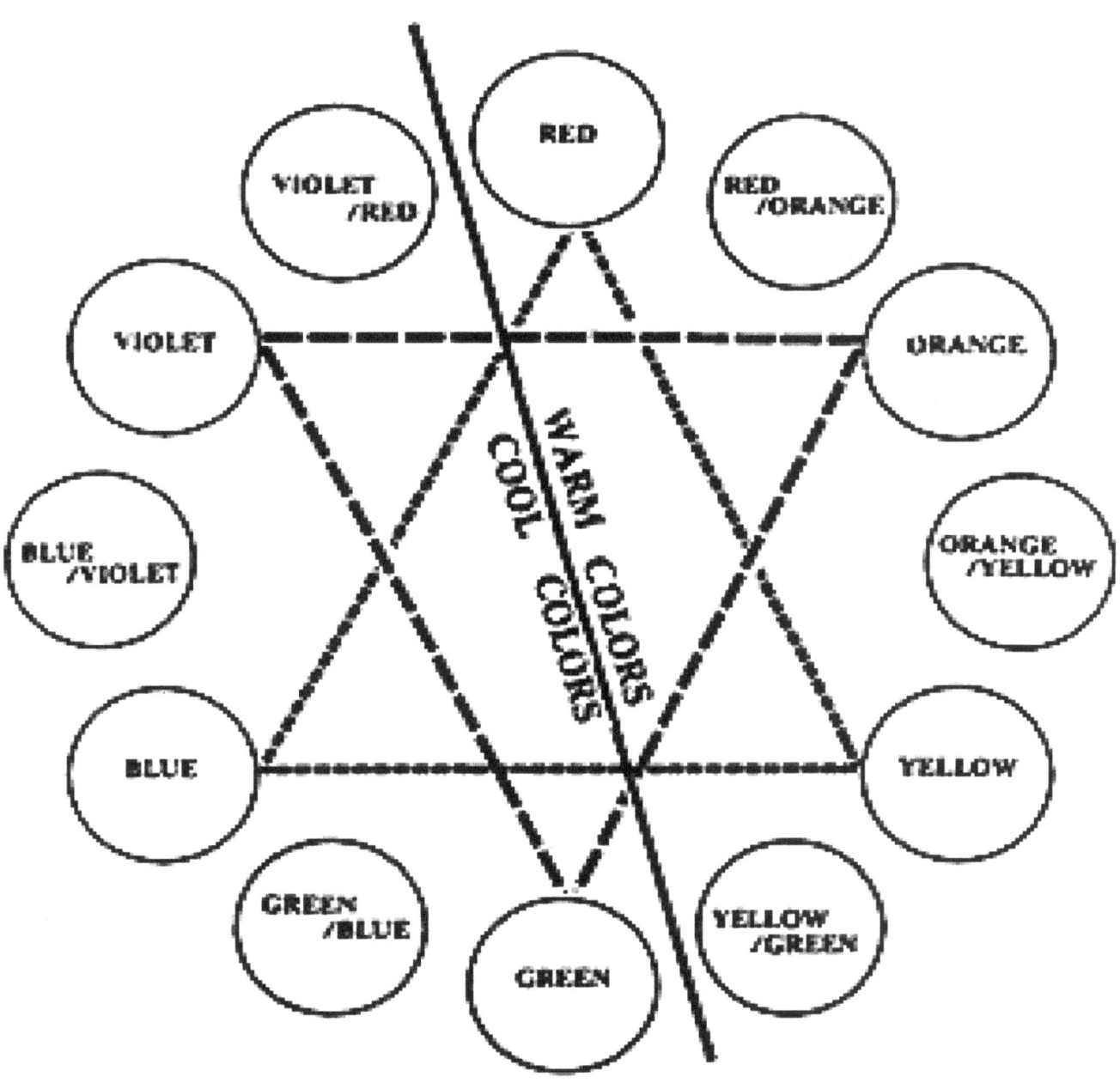

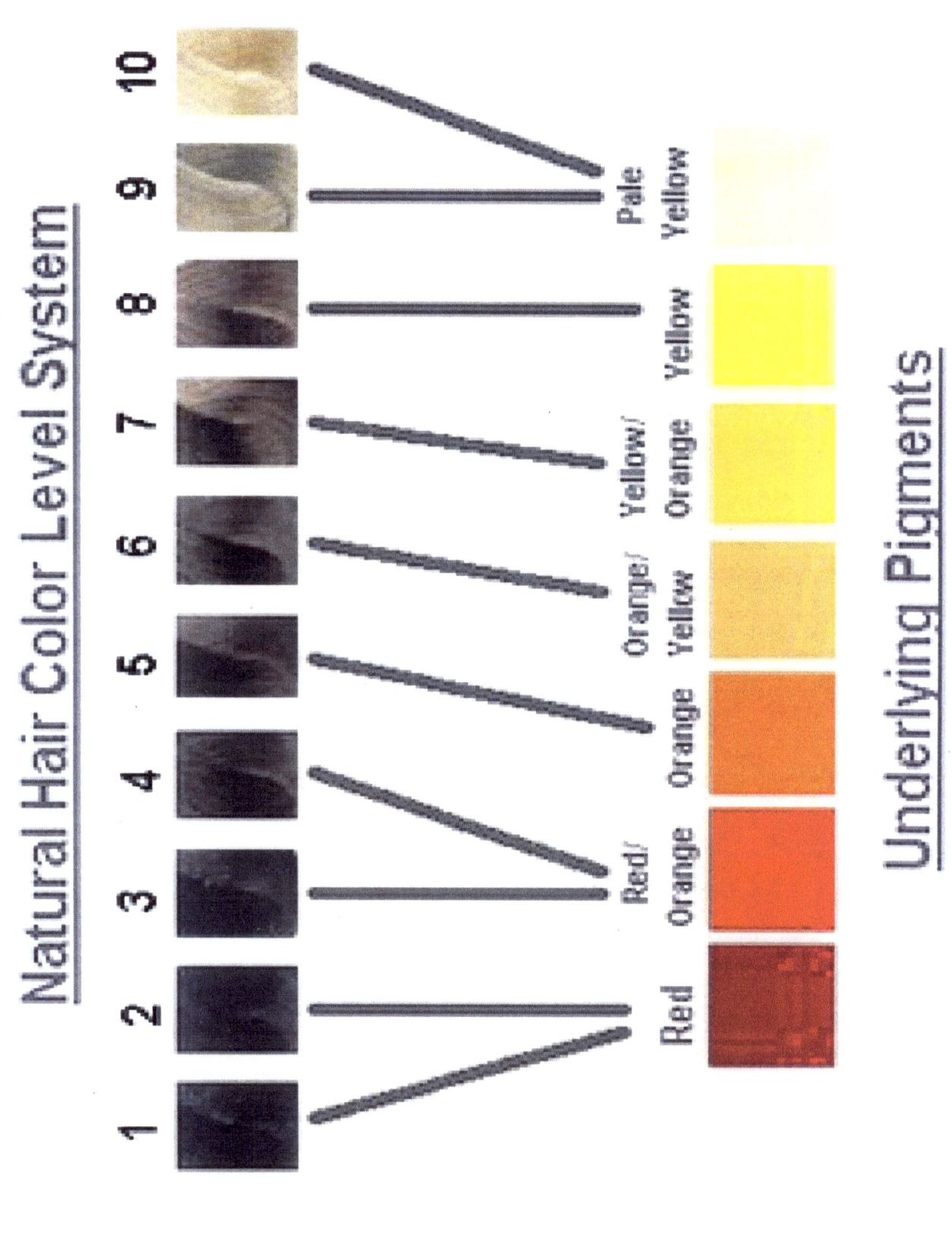

NOTES

NOTES

NOTES

NOTES

NOTES

NOTES

NOTES

NOTES

NOTES

NOTES

NOTES

NOTES

NOTES

NOTES

NOTES

NOTES

NOTES

NOTES

NOTES

NOTES

NOTES

www.ingramcontent.com/pod-product-compliance
Lightning Source LLC
Chambersburg PA
CBHW041526220426
43670CB00002B/46